Dirt

by Steve "The Dirtmeister" Tomecek

Illustrated by Nancy Woodman

NATIONAL GEOGRAPHIC

WASHINGTON, D.C.

Have you ever dug in the dirt?
Have you ever made mud pies?
Have you ever helped plant a garden?
You've probably noticed that not all dirt
looks the same.

Some dirt is dark in color. Some is light.
Some dirt is really sticky. Some is soft and
fluffy. Dirt in all its different forms is
important to our world. Let's dig into
the story of dirt and find out
what it's all about.

90.234

Some people think that dirt is just something to be cleaned up—like the stuff you wash out of your clothes. But dirt is really one of the most important things on Earth.

Scientists call dirt "soil."
Soil is found on the surface
of Earth. Soil is as important to life
on Earth as air or water. Without it,
many living things would die.

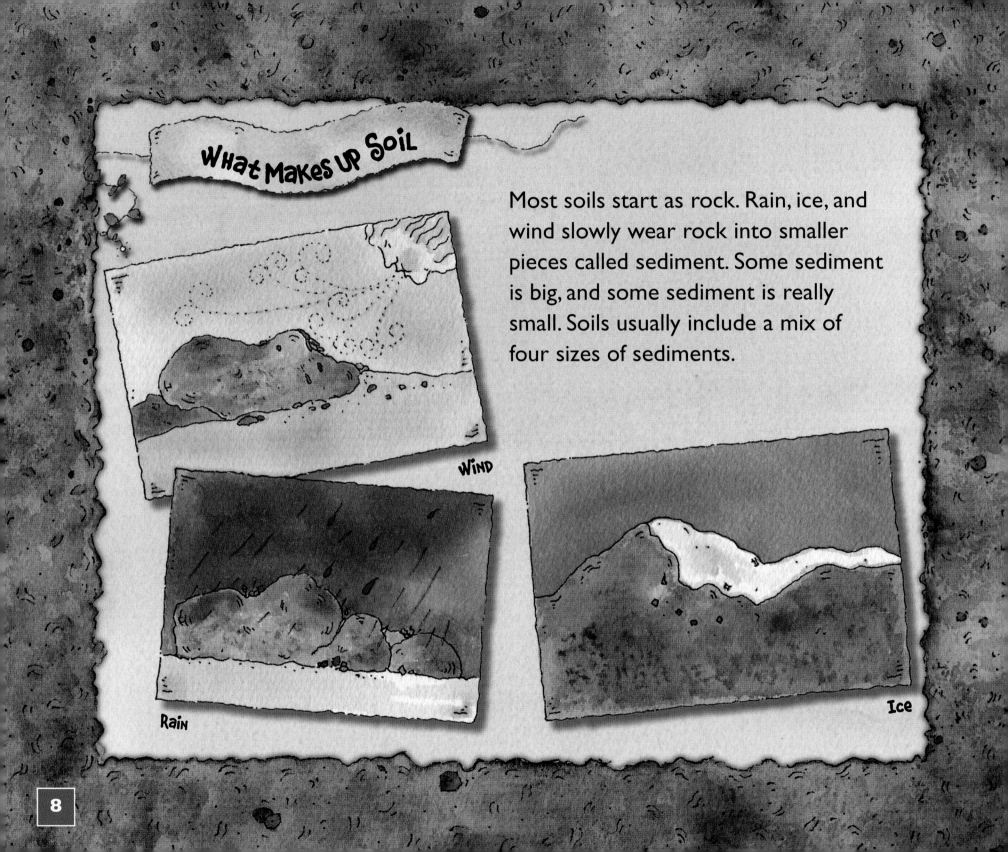

What Makes up Soil

Most soils start as rock. Rain, ice, and wind slowly wear rock into smaller pieces called sediment. Some sediment is big, and some sediment is really small. Soils usually include a mix of four sizes of sediments.

Wind

Rain

Ice

Gravel is the biggest sediment. It looks like small rocks. Grains of sand are about the size of grains of sugar. Sand makes the soil feel gritty. Silt feels like flour. Its grains are smaller than sand. Clay grains are tiny. When clay is wet, it makes soil really sticky. When clay is dry, it forms hard clumps.

Each type of soil has a different mix of sediments. These sediments all affect how water will act in soil. Have you ever spilled a drink on the sand at the beach? It sinks right in! Water usually flows right through sandy soils. If you plant a garden in sandy soil, you have to water it often.

Water has a hard time flowing through clay. Soils that have a great deal of clay often have puddles form on top of them when it rains. The best soils have an even mix of sand, silt, and clay.

SAND

Sediments in the soil are important because they give plant roots something to hold on to. If soils didn't have sediments, trees would fall over and buildings would sink into the ground. Sediments also contain minerals. Minerals help plants grow. Without minerals in the soil, most plants would die.

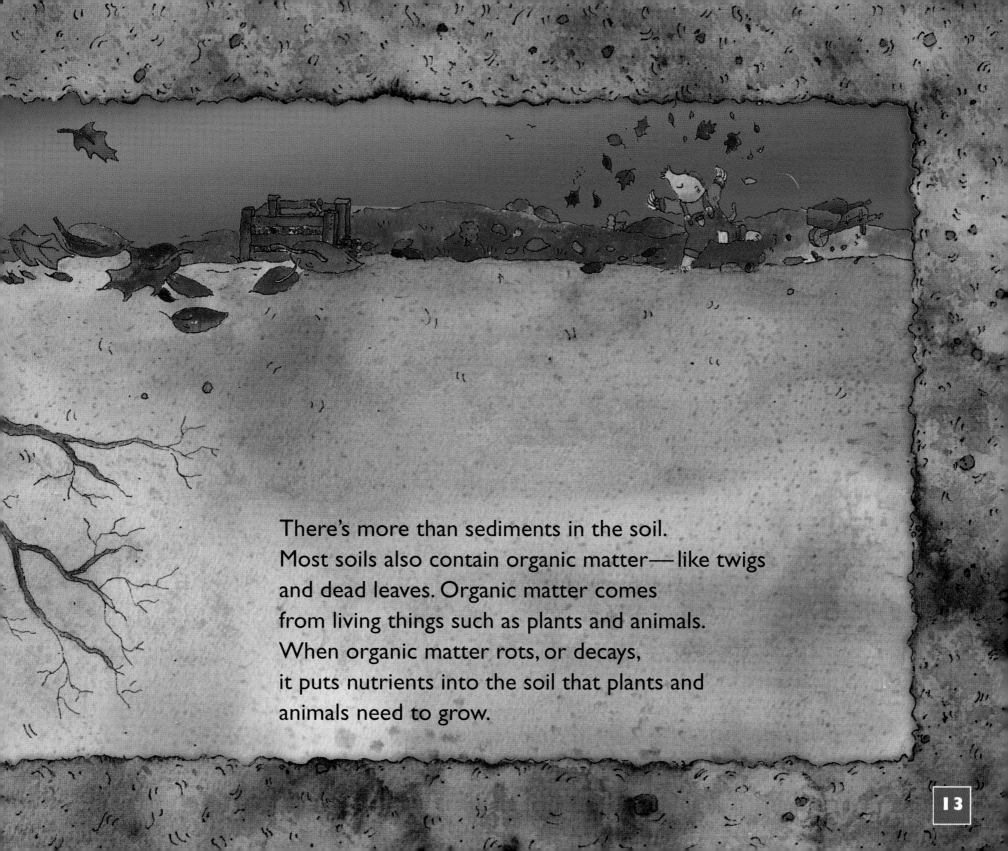

There's more than sediments in the soil.
Most soils also contain organic matter—like twigs
and dead leaves. Organic matter comes
from living things such as plants and animals.
When organic matter rots, or decays,
it puts nutrients into the soil that plants and
animals need to grow.

What Lives in Soil

CLOSE-UP
VIEW OF
MICROBES

Plants aren't the only things that live
in soil. Just one square foot of
good forest soil can be home to as many
as 300,000 different living things!

Critters such as insects, snakes, and moles live in the soil. Thousands of different microbes live there, too. Microbes are living things that are too tiny to see without a microscope, so you might not even know that they're there.

Some of the most important creatures found in the soil are earthworms. Earthworms eat organic matter attached to tiny pieces of sediment. To get their food, they swallow large amounts of dirt. When it comes out the other end, the soil is loose and fluffy and enriched with nutrients.

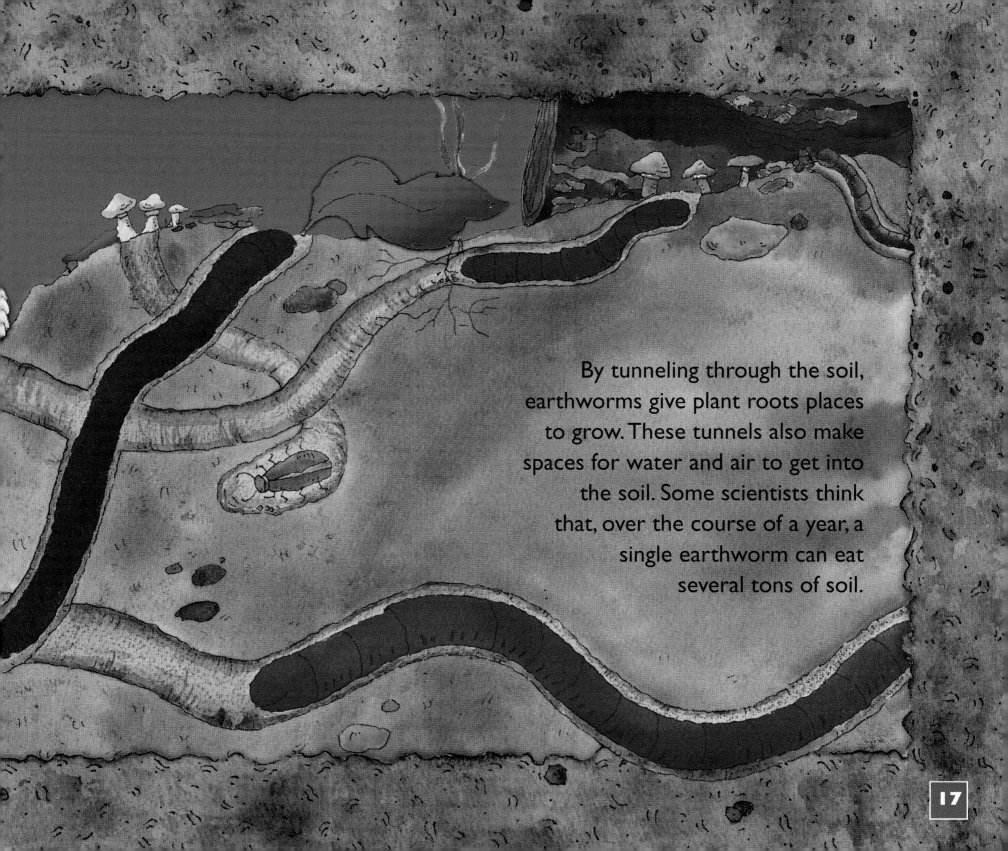

By tunneling through the soil, earthworms give plant roots places to grow. These tunnels also make spaces for water and air to get into the soil. Some scientists think that, over the course of a year, a single earthworm can eat several tons of soil.

17

Soil Helps things Grow

Earthworms don't do all the work. Insects and microbes may not sound too important, but they help make life possible for you. They help to recycle nutrients in the soil. Those nutrients help plants grow, and plants provide the food and oxygen you need to live.

When you eat a banana, a peanut butter sandwich, or even a hamburger, you owe your meal to the soil. That's right—even though a cow does not grow in the soil, it eats grass. If the grass didn't get nutrients from the soil to grow, you wouldn't have a glass of milk to drink!

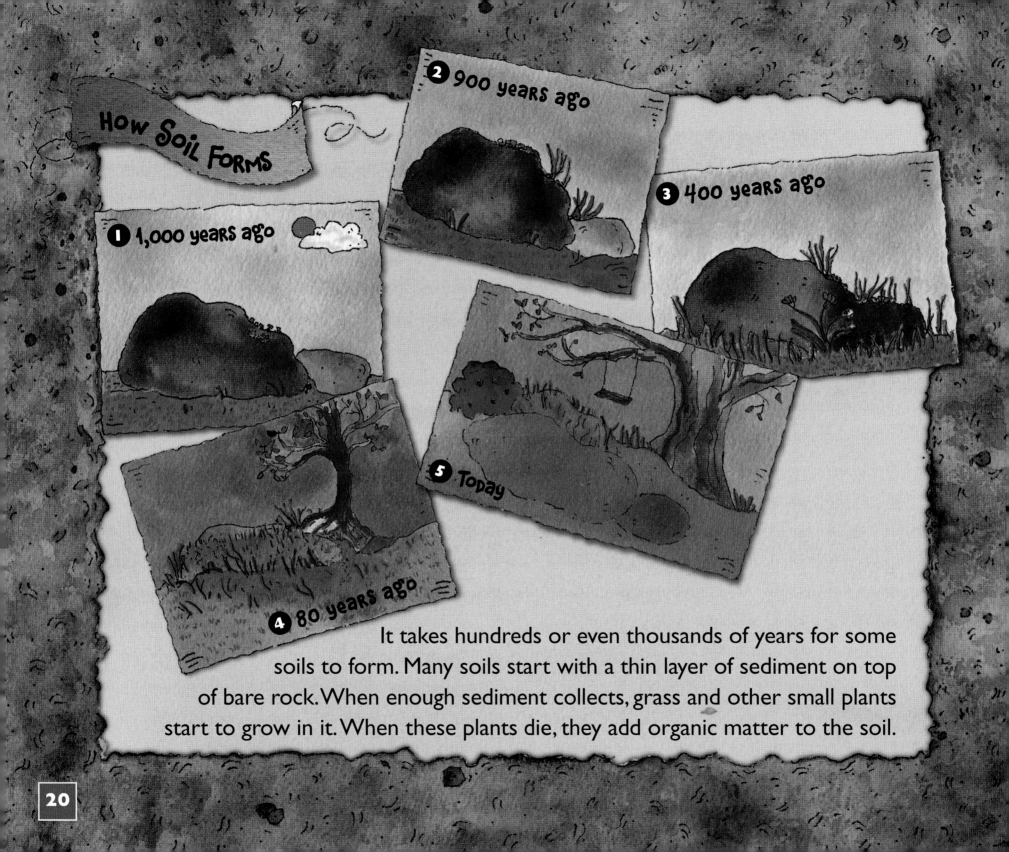

How Soil Forms

1 1,000 years ago

2 900 years ago

3 400 years ago

4 80 years ago

5 Today

It takes hundreds or even thousands of years for some soils to form. Many soils start with a thin layer of sediment on top of bare rock. When enough sediment collects, grass and other small plants start to grow in it. When these plants die, they add organic matter to the soil.

Sometimes living things make soil. Lichens are living things that grow on bare rock. As they grow, lichens slowly break the surface of the rock into sediment. Over hundreds of years, lichens make enough soil for other plants to grow.

Layers of Soil

Over time, sediment piles up to make different layers of soil. Scientists call these layers horizons. Each horizon looks different and has its own special features. By studying the different horizons, soil scientists can figure out how old a soil is and how it formed.

The fluffy, dark brown, top layer is called humus. It's made up mostly of dead plants and leaves. Under this is the topsoil. It's usually a rich, brown color. Below that is the red or yellow subsoil. The lowest horizon is called the parent material because it's made up of rocks and sediments that have broken down to form the other soil layers. Let's see how these four layers work together underground.

Humus

Topsoil

Subsoil

Parent Material

The humus has lots of organic matter. Many insects and worms live here because it is full of dead and decaying plants. It's where the nutrients get recycled and returned to the soil.

The topsoil is important for plants because it's the layer where they put their roots. Farmers want good, rich topsoil so their crops can grow fast and strong.

The subsoil is usually heavy and hard to dig in because it has a lot more clay in it. The subsoil has almost no organic matter. When people build homes with basements, they usually dig right into the subsoil.

The parent material is rocky and hard. Much of the time, building foundations are placed in the parent material because it provides the best support.

Soils Have Different Uses

By studying the different soil horizons, soil scientists can tell how old a soil is and where it came from and can make suggestions on how a soil might be used. Soils with thick, rich topsoil can be used for planting. Soils that have a hard, compact subsoil are ideal foundations for roads and parking lots.

Around the world, soil scientists have discovered more than 100,000 different types of soil! Sometimes it's hard to tell where one soil ends and another begins, so scientists make special soil maps to show where different soils are. By using soil maps and following the suggestions of soil scientists, people can select the best use for their soil.

MOLE'S SOIL MAP

garden Humus

Swimming Hole

Topsoil

Sand

Parent material

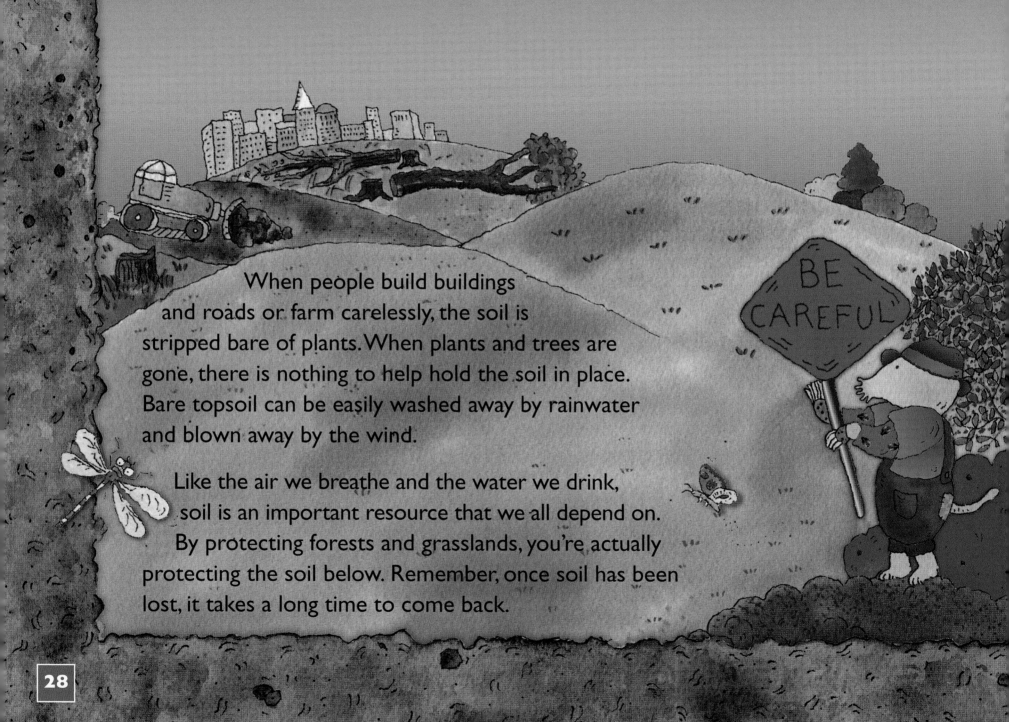

When people build buildings
and roads or farm carelessly, the soil is
stripped bare of plants. When plants and trees are
gone, there is nothing to help hold the soil in place.
Bare topsoil can be easily washed away by rainwater
and blown away by the wind.

Like the air we breathe and the water we drink,
soil is an important resource that we all depend on.
By protecting forests and grasslands, you're actually
protecting the soil below. Remember, once soil has been
lost, it takes a long time to come back.

BE CAREFUL

So next time you're munching on an apple or an ear of corn, don't forget to think about the soil. After all, dirt made your dinner!

Life in a Bottle

A Soil Ecosystem at Play

You can make your own model soil ecosystem.

Here's what you'll need:
a clean, clear plastic
2-liter soda bottle
★
4 cups of garden soil*
★
scissors
★
some grass seed or
wild bird seed
★
a spray bottle of water
★
a large rubber band
★
6-inch square of cloth

Do NOT use potting soil from a store!

1. Have an adult cut the top off the soda bottle about 8 inches from the bottom.

2. Find an organic garden area or a forest where you can dig about 4 cups of natural soil.

3. Put the soil in the cut-off bottle. Smooth it out with the spoon.

4. Sprinkle a small amount of seed on the soil. Spray lightly with water.

Every three days take the
cloth cover off the bottle
and give the soil a light
spray with water. Make
sure you put the
cloth back on
when you're done.

5. Cover the top of the bottle
with the cloth, and use the rubber
band to hold it on tight.

6. Place the bottle
near a window and watch
what happens inside.

What Did you Discover?

Use a mirror to read

In a few days, you
should start to see the
seeds sprout. Watch as
the roots make their
way down into the soil.
If you're lucky, you may
even notice several
different types of
insects in the soil. You
can even keep a
notebook to record
what happens inside
your soil ecosystem.

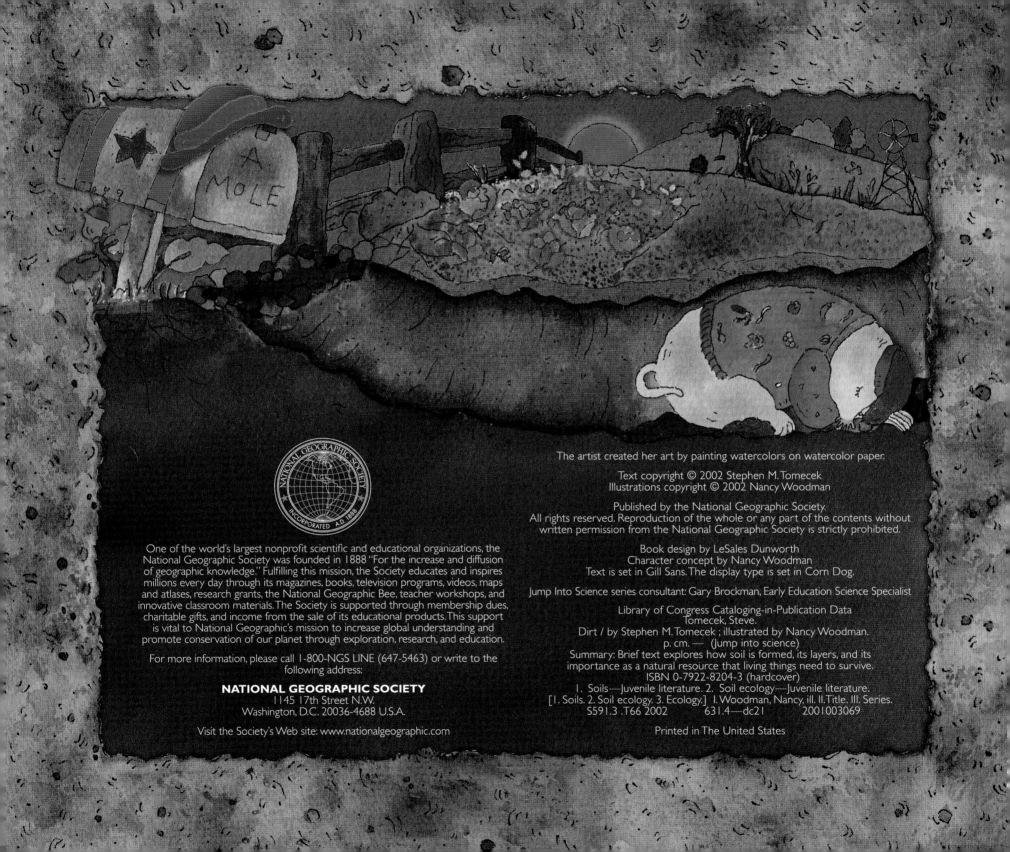

Text copyright © 2002 Stephen M. Tomecek
Illustrations copyright © 2002 Nancy Woodman

Published by the National Geographic Society.

Book design by LeSales Dunworth
Character concept by Nancy Woodman
Text is set in Gill Sans. The display type is set in Corn Dog.

Jump Into Science series consultant: Gary Brockman, Early Education Science Specialist

Library of Congress Cataloging-in-Publication Data
Tomecek, Steve.
Dirt / by Stephen M. Tomecek ; illustrated by Nancy Woodman.
p. cm. — (Jump into science)
Summary: Brief text explores how soil is formed, its layers, and its
importance as a natural resource that living things need to survive.
ISBN 0-7922-8204-3 (hardcover)
1. Soils—Juvenile literature. 2. Soil ecology—Juvenile literature.
[1. Soils. 2. Soil ecology. 3. Ecology.] I. Woodman, Nancy, ill. II. Title. III. Series.
S591.3 .T66 2002   631.4—dc21   2001003069

Printed in The United States

One of the world's largest nonprofit scientific and educational organizations, the
National Geographic Society was founded in 1888 "For the increase and diffusion
of geographic knowledge." Fulfilling this mission, the Society educates and inspires
millions every day through its magazines, books, television programs, videos, maps
and atlases, research grants, the National Geographic Bee, teacher workshops, and
innovative classroom materials. The Society is supported through membership dues,
charitable gifts, and income from the sale of its educational products. This support
is vital to National Geographic's mission to increase global understanding and
promote conservation of our planet through exploration, research, and education.

For more information, please call 1-800-NGS LINE (647-5463) or write to the
following address:

NATIONAL GEOGRAPHIC SOCIETY
1145 17th Street N.W.
Washington, D.C. 20036-4688 U.S.A.

Visit the Society's Web site: www.nationalgeographic.com